The READ AGAIN & AGAIN New TESTAMENT BIBLE STORYBOOK

ILLUSTRATED BY CHRIS JONES

FOCUS ON THE FAMILY.

A Focus on the Family
resource published by
Tyndale House Publishers

The Read Again and Again New Testament Bible Storybook

Copyright © 2024 Focus on the Family. All rights reserved.

A Focus on the Family book published by Tyndale House Publishers, Carol Stream, Illinois 60188

Focus on the Family and the accompanying logo and design are federally registered trademarks of Focus on the Family, 8605 Explorer Drive, Colorado Springs, CO 80920.

Tyndale and Tyndale's quill logo are registered trademarks of Tyndale House Ministries.

Design by Lexie Rhodes and Mike Harrigan

Cover and interior illustrations by Chris Jones

All Scripture quotations, unless otherwise indicated, are taken from the Holy Bible, *New International Reader's Version*®, *NIrV*.® Copyright © 1995, 1996, 1998, 2014 by Biblica, Inc.® Used by permission. All rights reserved worldwide.

The material in this book originally appeared in *Focus on the Family Clubhouse Jr.* magazine.

For manufacturing information regarding this product, please call 1-855-277-9400.

For information about special discounts for bulk purchases, please contact Tyndale House Publishers at csresponse@tyndale.com, or call 1-855-277-9400.

ISBN 978-1-64607-138-8

Printed in China

30	29	28	27	26	25	24
7	6	5	4	3	2	1

The READ AGAIN & AGAIN New Testament Bible StoryBook

ILLUSTRATED BY
CHRIS JONES

"Let the little children come to me.

Don't keep them away.

God's kingdom belongs

to people like them."

MARK 10:14

TABLE OF CONTENTS

WELCOME, PARENTS!

Now more than ever, kids need to be equipped with the truth of the Bible from a young age. For more than thirty-five years, *Focus on the Family Clubhouse Jr.* magazine has helped children engage with their faith and learn what it means to be a follower of Jesus.

This book contains New Testament Bible stories originally published in the pages of *Clubhouse Jr.* These visually engaging

stories were designed to grab your children's attention—the kinds of stories that kids will want to read again and again. As an added benefit, most of these stories feature a question or short takeaway for you to discuss together. Our goal is to help your children apply what they learn.

We pray that as your kids hear these stories, they'll grow in their love of Jesus, their knowledge of the Bible, and their understanding of how God calls us to live—and love. We hope your entire family wants to read them again and again!

Blessings,
Jesse Florea
Editor, *Clubhouse Jr.*

by Jacqueline Cotton • based on Luke 1

Something to Talk About

"**G**ood morning, Rabbi Zechariah!" Joanna called as she
carried her water bucket to the well.
Instead of saying "Hello!" like he usually did, Zechariah just waved.
"Is something wrong?" Joanna asked.
Zechariah smiled and shook his head.
Maybe he lost his voice, Joanna thought.

"**M**ama, why doesn't Rabbi Zechariah talk anymore?" Joanna asked when she got home. "Is he sick?"

"No," Mama said. "But he hasn't said a word since he returned from the temple."

"It sounds like a mystery," Joanna said. "Can I try to solve it?"

"OK," Mama said. "But don't go snooping too much."

Joanna carefully watched Rabbi Zechariah's house. For months, she never saw him speak to anyone. And Joanna never saw his wife, Elizabeth, outside anymore.

Strange, Joanna thought.

One day a young woman came to visit Zechariah and Elizabeth. Elizabeth looked happy to see the girl.

"Thank you for coming, Mary," Elizabeth exclaimed. "My baby just jumped inside me!"

Joanna ran home.

"They're going to have a baby," she told Mama.

"How exciting!" Mama said. "They've wanted a baby ever since we've been their neighbors. Children are a gift from God."

A few months later, the baby was born. Everyone visited Elizabeth and Zechariah to congratulate them.

When Joanna walked inside their home, some people were arguing about the baby's name.

"He must be called John," Elizabeth said. "An angel gave us the name. At first my husband didn't believe. That's why Zechariah hasn't been able to speak."

"You saw an angel?" Joanna asked.

Everyone looked at Zechariah. He grabbed a tablet and wrote: *His name is John.*

"Yes, child," Zechariah said, happy to be able to talk again.

HIS NAME IS JOHN

Pointing the Way
Zechariah and Elizabeth's son grew up to be John the Baptist. Elizabeth's cousin, Mary, was Jesus' mother! When John grew up, he had an important job. He told people about Jesus—God's greatest gift of all.

FAITH and TRUST

by Catherine Osornio • based on Luke 2:1-7

Knock! Knock! Knock!

Joseph stared at the wooden door. He and Mary had been all over Bethlehem. Roman authorities had ordered people to return to their hometowns. Now all the inns were full. Would this place turn them away too?

Bang! Bang! Bang! Joseph knocked harder.

Mary sat patiently on a donkey. She was tired and in pain. The trip from Nazareth had been difficult, especially because she was about to have a baby.

Let them have room for us, Lord, Joseph prayed. *Otherwise the Messiah might be born in the street.*

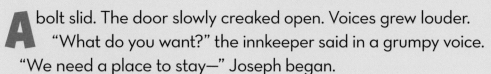

A bolt slid. The door slowly creaked open. Voices grew louder.

"What do you want?" the innkeeper said in a grumpy voice.

"We need a place to stay—" Joseph began.

"We're full!" *Slam! Click!*

Joseph walked slowly back to Mary. He led the donkey down the road. Only one inn was left. Perhaps it would have a room.

It looked crowded, but Joseph had to try.

Knock! Knock! Knock!

Lord, please! he prayed.

THANK YOU!

I HAVE A STABLE. THAT'S ALL I CAN OFFER.

The door opened. A man stared at Joseph.

"Sir," Joseph said, "my wife is about to have a baby. We need somewhere to stay."

The innkeeper looked exhausted. "There's no room here."

"Please, sir!" Joseph said earnestly. "We'll take anything!"

"I have a stable," the man said. "In the back. There is fresh hay and some blankets. That's all I can offer."

"Thank you!" Joseph said out loud. *Thank You, Lord!* he thought happily.

The stable was full of animals. Joseph cleared a space for Mary. She looked relieved to be resting.

"Where will we put the baby?" she asked.

Joseph looked around. He had carved a beautiful cradle, but it was at their home in Nazareth. All Joseph could find was a stone manger that held the animals' food.

Once again, Lord, You have provided, Joseph prayed.

He cleaned out the manger and placed fresh straw inside.

Soon, animal noises were joined by a baby's cry.

The Savior was here at last!

Mary wrapped Him in cloths and laid Him in the manger.

"Welcome, baby Jesus!" Joseph said softly.

A Trustworthy Man
Joseph was faithful. He trusted God and stayed loyal to His plan. God spoke to Joseph in his dreams, and Joseph always obeyed God's directions. Do you always obey? Do you keep your promises? Ask God to help you become faithful like Joseph.

A JOYOUS DAY

by Danika Cooley • based on Luke 2:22-40

Mary tightly wrapped her baby boy in a blanket. She picked up Jesus and cradled Him in her arms.

"I'm ready to go," Mary said.

Joseph smiled. He helped Mary onto the back of their donkey. Slowly, they began the 5 mile journey from Bethlehem to Jerusalem.

Today was the big day. Mary and Joseph were taking their baby to the temple to dedicate Him to the Lord.

Over in Jerusalem, Simeon's neighbor called to him, "Where are you going this morning?"

"To the temple to see God's promised gift!" Simeon said.

"You say that almost every morning," his neighbor teased.

"God's timing is perfect," Simeon replied. "And He promised I'd see the Messiah before I die."

Simeon made the short trip to the temple. As he passed through the gates, gray-haired Anna was already there worshiping God.

"Praise be to the Lord God of Israel, who loves His people!" she sang.

Mary and Joseph looked around in excitement as they brought baby Jesus into the temple.

Simeon quickly stepped forward. The Holy Spirit helped him recognize God's Son.

"Lord, You are the King over all," he said, taking Jesus into his arms.

Simeon had waited his whole life to see the Messiah. Now he looked at baby Jesus and prayed to God, "My eyes have seen Your salvation. You have prepared it in the sight of all people."

Mary and Joseph looked at their baby and then at each other with wide eyes.

Just then, Anna hurried over to see Jesus. Her heart filled with joy at the sight of the special baby who would rescue God's people. Anna praised God and told everyone around her about Jesus.

Mary held Jesus close. "What a baby we have," she said to Joseph.

Joseph nodded. "He is the reason to celebrate."

"A child will be born to us. . . .
He will rule over us. And he will be called
Wonderful Adviser and Mighty God."
—Isaiah 9:6

Welcoming Jesus

When Simeon and Anna saw Jesus, they praised God. How can you praise God this week? Jesus came to forgive us of our sins—and that's a great reason to celebrate.

13

by Jacqui L. Hershberger • based on Matthew 2

Wise Moves

When Jesus was born, a star appeared just for Him! The star was God's sign that His Son had come to earth. Wise men followed the star to Jerusalem. They went to the palace and told King Herod they were searching for the child who was born to be king.

Herod grew very upset that a new king might replace him. But he pretended he wanted to worship the future king. He told the wise men to find Jesus and tell him where the child lived.

The wise men went to Bethlehem. They followed the star to Joseph and Mary's home. Then they gave Jesus gifts of gold, frankincense and myrrh.

In a dream, God warned the wise men not to tell King Herod where Jesus lived. They went home a different way, without saying a word to Herod.

When the wise men left, Joseph also had a dream. The angel of the Lord told him, "Get up! Take the child and His mother and escape to Egypt until I tell you to come back. Herod is going to search for the child. He wants to kill Him."

Joseph obeyed right away. He woke up Mary, and they started the long trip to Egypt.

Later, Herod realized the wise men had tricked him. He was very mad. But Jesus had already escaped!

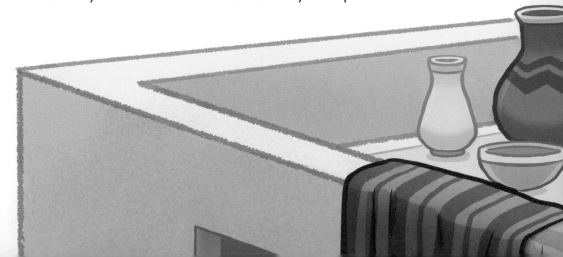

After King Herod died, Joseph had another dream. This time, the angel of the Lord told him to move his family back to Israel.

When they reached Israel, Joseph heard that Herod's son had become king. Joseph worried that Herod's son might try to kill Jesus. After being warned in another dream, Joseph settled his family safely in the town of Nazareth.

Right Away

Joseph obeyed right away each time God told him to do something. He didn't complain—even when he moved his family in the middle of the night! Joseph's obedience kept baby Jesus safe.

When your parents ask you to do something, remember Joseph and obey right away. Your quick obedience will help keep you safe, too!

BOY WONDER

by Jacqui L. Hershberger • based on Luke 2:41-50

SUCH WISDOM FOR ONE SO YOUNG!

Dotan followed his rabbi up the temple steps. Crowds of people had come to Jerusalem to celebrate Passover.

Just then, a teacher of the law hurried to meet them.

"Have you heard the boy in the temple?" the teacher asked. "We can't believe the questions He asks or the answers He gives. Such wisdom for one so young!"

Dotan quickly followed the older men into the temple courtyard.

The rabbis and teachers of the law gathered around a boy. Dotan had never seen Him before.

What's so special about Him? Dotan wondered.

"His name is Jesus," a rabbi whispered. One of the teachers asked Jesus a question.

Dotan thought about the answer he would give. He was pretty sure he had it right. But Jesus gave an answer that made the rabbis twirl their beards in thought.

Next, Jesus asked a hard question. For the rest of that day and the next two days, Jesus and the rabbis discussed God's law. Dotan liked how Jesus' questions made him understand new things about God.

On the third day, a man and woman rushed up to Jesus. They looked worried and pulled Jesus away from the group.

They must be His parents, Dotan thought.

DIDN'T YOU KNOW I HAD TO BE IN MY FATHER'S HOUSE?

Then Dotan heard Jesus say, "Didn't you know I had to be in my Father's house?"

What does He mean? Dotan wondered.

Over the next 20 years, Dotan studied hard and became a teacher of the law. He wanted to understand as much about God as he could.

One day, a friend asked if he'd heard the new teacher.

"His name is Jesus," the friend said. "He heals people and tells stories that explain great truths about God."

That must be the same Jesus I heard in the temple, Dotan thought.

"He claims that He's the Son of God!" A nearby Pharisee snorted in disgust.

I WANT TO HEAR HIM TEACH.

Looking for Truth

Would you like to learn more about Jesus, too? Your parents can help you search God's Word for answers. God reveals truth and gives wisdom to those who ask (James 1:5).

The Son of God? Dotan tugged his beard. He remembered what Jesus had said many years ago about the temple being His "Father's house."

Could Jesus really be God's Son? Dotan wondered. That would explain how well He understood the Scriptures.

"I want to hear Him teach," Dotan said. "I must find out the truth about Jesus for myself."

by Becky Wilson Suggs • based on Matthew 3:1-12

LEADING THE WAY

I HEARD HE EATS LOCUSTS AND HONEY.

Shhhhh, CHILDREN.

YUCK!

Abigail and Asher stood with their parents on the banks of the Jordan River. They had come to hear John the Baptist speak. John wasn't an ordinary man. He was a powerful preacher for God. He lived in the wilderness and wore clothes made of camel's hair. Many people followed John and wanted to hear what he had to say.

"I heard he eats locusts and honey," Asher whispered to Abigail.

"Yuck!" she giggled.

"Shhhhh, children," Father said. "This man has an important message for us from God."

Abigail and Asher listened closely. John's words were different than the lessons they heard in the temple.

"Turn from your sins and follow God," John told the crowd. "Then be baptized to show everyone you follow God's way."

Not everyone liked what John said. Some leaders from the temple crossed their arms and frowned at him.

23

Abigail pulled on her father's cloak. He knelt down.

"Why don't the religious leaders like John?" she asked.

Their father smiled. "Do you remember the words of Isaiah we heard at the temple?" he asked.

Abigail and Asher shook their heads.

"He said God would send someone to prepare the way for the Messiah, the Savior of the world," he said. "But some religious leaders follow rules, instead of following God."

"John is making sure everyone is ready for the Messiah," their mother explained. "Your father and I are ready to follow Him."

The children looked at each other and smiled. "I want to follow God and be baptized too," Asher said.

"Me too!" Abigail exclaimed. "Even though John is a little different, I believe what he is saying."

They all prayed together. Their family was choosing to follow God and show the world they loved Him.

Asher and Abigail held hands as they stepped into the river. As John reached out to them, they smiled. They knew they were choosing to follow the right leader.

Loving Leadership
Jesus proved He was the Messiah by fulfilling Old Testament prophecies and rising from the dead. Who do you follow? The best leaders aren't the ones with the coolest toys or best birthday parties. Instead, good leaders, like John, point to Jesus and encourage you to grow stronger in Him.

by Crystal Bowman and Teri McKinley • based on Matthew 7:7-12

SNAKES AND STONES

Benjamin sat on the grass next to his sister, Elizabeth. They listened as Jesus talked to a big crowd of people.

"Suppose your son asks for bread," Jesus said. "Which of you will give him a stone? Or suppose he asks for a fish. Which of you will give him a snake?"

Benjamin laughed at the idea of his mom serving stones for dinner. Elizabeth giggled too.

"Quiet down," their dad whispered, but he was grinning too.

Jesus smiled at the laughter.

"You know how to give good gifts to your children," He continued. "How much more will your Father who is in heaven give good gifts."

On the walk home, Benjamin kept thinking about the things Jesus said. *Eating a stone would be impossible.* He laughed. *And fish is way better than a snake.*

An idea popped into Benjamin's head for a joke. He found four gray stones and put them in his sack. Next, he found a curvy black stick that was shaped like a snake.

"Perfect!" he whispered to himself.

"Hurry up, Benjamin," his mom called from ahead.

"Coming!" Benjamin yelled.

At home, the smell of fresh bread soon filled the house.

"Put this on the table," Mom said, handing Benjamin a basket of bread.

Benjamin set the basket on the table and placed the stones in the basket. Then he put the curvy stick next to the basket.

When everyone sat down for dinner, Elizabeth screamed. "Eeeekk! A snake!"

"It's just a stick," Dad said with a laugh. He pulled a stone out of the bread basket and knocked it against the table. "This bread is as hard as a rock!"

Mom looked at Benjamin. "Did you put these stones and this stick on the table?"

"I did," Benjamin said. "Jesus talked about giving snakes and stones instead of bread and fish. It was funny, so I wanted to make a joke."

Dad patted Benjamin on the head. "What do you think Jesus meant when He said that?" he asked.

Benjamin shrugged his shoulders.

"Would I give you stones and a snake if you asked me for bread and fish?" Dad asked.

Benjamin shook his head.

"Then what kind of gifts do you think God gives His children?" Dad said.

Benjamin smiled. "Good ones!"

"Exactly," Mom said, holding up a rock. "Now eat your dinner."

"No thanks." Benjamin smiled. "Your food tastes much better!"

A Good Father

Your parents want what's best for you. Jesus wanted the people to know that God was a good Father who loved them. Good fathers don't give their kids everything they ask for, but they do give their kids good gifts.

by Karen Witemeyer • based on Matthew 18:1-14

Not Too Little

"**J**esus is here! Jesus is here!" Nathan dropped the beetle he had just picked off the ground. He looked toward the excited voices. He had heard of Jesus, the man of God who could do miracles. How amazing it would be to see Him in person!

Dozens of men and women headed toward the lake. Nathan followed. But with such a huge crowd, he couldn't see a thing.

He tried jumping. That didn't work. He tried squeezing between people, but there were too many.

Nathan tugged on a tall man's sleeve.

"Stop that," the man said. "I'm trying to hear Jesus."

Nathan turned to a woman. "Can you help me, please? I want to get closer to Jesus."

The woman laughed. "Go play with your friends," she said. "You're too little to understand the Master's teachings."

Nathan sighed and turned to one more person. "Excuse me, sir. Can you help me see Jesus?"

The man frowned. "Children have no place here. Go home."

Tears filled Nathan's eyes. Embarrassed and hurt, he ducked behind a tree. *Why won't anyone help me?* he wondered. *Did Jesus only care about grown-ups?*

Nathan heard voices from the other side of the tree.

"Jesus," they said, "who is the most important person in Your kingdom?"

Nathan peeked out. The crowd had shifted. A path opened through the middle, and Nathan found himself looking at Jesus.

"Come here, child," Jesus called. Nathan bit his bottom lip and moved on wobbly legs. Everyone stared, and Nathan wanted to hide again.

Jesus smiled at him. He placed His hands on Nathan's shoulders and faced the crowd.

"**Y**ou need to change and become like little children," Jesus said. "Anyone who takes the humble position of this child is the most important in the kingdom of heaven. Anyone who welcomes a little child like this in My name welcomes Me."

The more Jesus spoke, the better Nathan felt. Then Jesus knelt in front of him and spoke in a low voice. "My Father God and I love you more than you could ever imagine," He said. "Thank you for helping Me today."

Nathan hurried to tell his mother what had happened. As he ran past the people who wouldn't help him, he smiled and waved. They had learned something about Jesus, and so had he. Jesus loved him and welcomed him. That was all he needed to know.

King of Pick-Up Sticks

by Christy Hoss • based on Mark 2:1-12

I love to play games. My friends and I don't have fancy games like they sell in the marketplace. We just play with what we find outside. Rocks and leaves are OK. But sticks are the best!

We look for thin, short sticks and put them in a pile. Then we take turns picking up one stick at a time. You have to be careful. If more than one stick moves, you lose your turn. When the pile is gone, the one with the most sticks is the winner.

I almost always win. That's why my friends call me the "King of Pick-Up Sticks."

This morning I'm playing at a friend's house.

Is that Jesus? I wonder as a man walks in. *When did He get back in town?*

More people follow Jesus. Pretty soon the house is packed. My parents show up, too. They say Jesus is the Messiah we've been waiting for.

People squish together. Everybody wants to hear Jesus. I find a spot on the ground in front of the adults. More and more people come.

While I wait, I pull out sticks from my satchel and pile them up.

Before I can pick the first one, Jesus starts speaking. Everyone hushes. It's easy to listen to Him, but I keep peeking down at my game.

Suddenly, dust and sticks rain down from the ceiling. We look up and see four men staring down through a hole in the roof. They begin to lower a man on a mat.

The man lands between me and Jesus. The man's legs are as skinny as sticks. I can tell he can't walk.

My heart beats hard. These men interrupted Jesus and dug a big hole in my neighbor's roof. I've gotten in trouble for much less than that.

But Jesus doesn't seem to mind. He speaks gently to the man. "Son, your sins are forgiven. Get up, take your mat and go home."

Then it happens. The man stands straight up! The crowd can't say a word. We're all amazed as we watch him walk out of the house.

I turn to look at Jesus. He kneels beside me. Without taking His eyes off mine, He pulls a stick from the pile. He doesn't even look! But not one stick moves. He stands, hands me the stick, smiles and begins teaching again.

Wow! I really want to play more with Jesus. But I know He has important things to do while He's here, like healing people and teaching us about God.

And I know something even more important.
My parents were right: Jesus is the Messiah.
He is the King of kings . . . and the true
"King of Pick-Up Sticks."

SONS OF THUNDER

by Catherine L. Osornio • based on Mark 3:17 and Luke 9:46-56

Thunder booms in the clouds. When you hear it, you know a storm is coming. Thunder can be scary. Some people and animals hide when they hear thunder.

My name is John. Not John the Baptist, I'm John the apostle. When Jesus met me and my brother James, He called us "Sons of Thunder." That's not a great nickname.

Jesus saw something in my brother and me that was shocking. Somehow He knew when we argued and got angry, look out!

Following Jesus changed our lives. He often had me, James and our friend, Peter, spend extra time with Him.

As we traveled with Jesus around Israel, we saw lots of miracles. Jesus healed the sick, fed thousands of people with a few loaves of bread and a couple fish and even brought dead people back to life!

Jesus became very popular. People followed Him everywhere. Because we were His closest friends, we started thinking we were special too. We all argued about who was the most important. Jesus stopped us, saying, "The one considered least important among all of you is really the most important."

After our argument, we came to a village in Samaria. James and I were still a little upset. A few of us went into the town. We expected the people to take good care of us. But no one wanted to sell us any food or offer us a place to stay!

That made me and my brother really angry. *How dare they treat us that way!* I thought.

We went to talk to Jesus.

"They don't want You to come into town," we said to Him. "We need to do something."

My brother and I knew the Scriptures. We remembered that Elijah the prophet was bothered by soldiers who wanted him to stop doing God's work. Elijah called down fire from heaven.

"Lord, do You want us to call down fire from heaven to destroy them?" we asked.

Jesus looked disappointed. I thought back to all the times He told us to love others and show forgiveness. Jesus didn't come to destroy people, but to rescue them.

He commanded us not to do it.

As we left to go to another village, we realized Jesus was right—about us and about showing love. The "Sons of Thunder" had to be more loving so people would see they needed Jesus to be their Savior. That was the most important thing of all.

Learning Self-Control
James and John often got angry. Jesus taught them it is better to be loving than angry. Ask God to help you control your temper so you can share Jesus' love with others too.

Eyes Wide Open

by Mike Nappa • based on Mark 10:46-52

> **JESUS IS HERE. HE'S REALLY HERE!**

When you close your eyes, you see what I see.
Nothing. Darkness.
But if you're like me, you hear everything.
You can almost taste the sunshine and smell the rain.
My name is Bartimaeus. I am blind.

ost days, I sit beside the road to Jericho. People walk by me as
they travel. It's usually not very exciting. But today,
something interesting is happening.

A large crowd surrounds me, and I hear whispering.

"He's coming!" they say. "Jesus is here. He's really here!"

I've heard of Jesus. If anyone can heal my blindness, it's the
Son of God.

"Jesus!" I shout. "Son of David! Have mercy on me!"

JESUS!

HAVE MERCY
ON ME!

"**Q**uiet!" someone tells me. "Jesus has a lot of other important things to do."
Everything I've heard about the Messiah makes me think He would have sympathy for me. I can't be quiet. This might be my only chance to talk to Jesus.
I start shouting louder.

"Jesus! Have mercy on me!"

Suddenly, I hear a voice. It must be Jesus!

"Come here," He says.

I jump to my feet. Some people guide me forward.

"What do you want Me to do for you?" Jesus asks.

"Teacher," I say, "I want to see."

"Your faith has healed you," He says.

I blink, and suddenly **I can see.**

I can see Jesus smiling at me.

Loving Others

Even though Jesus was busy teaching people about God, He always made time to help people in need. How can you show someone you know that you care?

A MIGHTY OFFERING

by Becky Wilson Suggs • based on Mark 12:41-44

CLANG!
CLANG
CLANG!

Coins dropped into the treasury box with a loud **CLANG**. My parents and I looked at each other as we stood in line at the temple.

"Josiah," Mama said, "do you remember why we give money at God's house?"

"God wants us to give back to Him," I said.

"That's right!" Mama smiled. "Giving back is a way to thank God for all He's given us. Plus, our gifts help others."

I nodded and clutched my coins, eager to give.

As each offering made a loud **CLANG**, I saw the giver walk away puffed with pride. Many looked rich in their fancy robes. Then I noticed an older lady in front of us. Her clothes were plain. I could see where she had mended her cloak.

"My name is Josiah." I smiled. "Is your family here, too?"

"My name is Sarah," she said, "and I'm alone. My husband is in heaven now."

"I'm sorry," I said.

eople talked. Pigeons cooed. But **CLANGING** coins made the most noise. Suddenly, Abba pointed. "There's Jesus!" he said. *Wow, He's here!* I thought. My family and I had listened to Him teach and seen Him heal the sick. Jesus and His disciples watched people give their offerings.

THERE'S JESUS!

inally, it was Sarah's turn. She walked up and dropped two small coins into the box. They barely made a tiny clink. Some people laughed and pointed. I started to get mad. Then I heard Jesus tell His disciples, "That poor widow has put more into the offering box than all the others. She put in everything she had."

Everything she had, I thought. *That's the most you can give!*

I turned to my parents. "Can we invite Sarah to share a meal with us?"

"Of course!" they said.

I hurried forward and put my coins in the offering box. Turning around, I grabbed my parents' hands and ran to catch up with Sarah.

Just a Mite

The small copper coins the widow gave were called **mites**. Though not worth much, the widow's offering meant more to Jesus than all the big offerings. How can we give Jesus all we have?

LIVING PROOF

by Christy Hoss • based on Luke 8:40-42, 49-56

Lying in bed, my eyelids feel heavy, like rocks are dragging them shut. I'm sick, and I don't have strength to keep them open.

My family surrounds the bed. I can hear their cries . . . except for Papa's. I heard him talking with my mother. He went to see a great teacher to ask for a miracle. My father is a leader at the synagogue, so he knows lots of important people.

I wish Papa was here, but I know he's doing what he believes is best for me. I just hope he returns quickly.

Suddenly, I no longer hear the sobs of those crying at my bed. Instead calm, peaceful sounds of joy fill the air. I'm surrounded by light and love.

Am I dreaming? I wonder.

Before I know the answer, I hear a voice say, "My child, get up."

My eyes flutter open. I'm back in my bed looking at the smile of a man. I've never seen him before, but somehow I know I truly am His child. My heart and life belong to Him.

His hand is warm. He gently helps me to my feet.

Papa dances around the room shouting, "Praise Jesus the Messiah!"

Mama cries tears of joy, pulling me into her arms. As she squeezes me tighter, I look over her shoulder at the One who took away my sickness.

"What happened?" I ask Papa. "What have I missed?"

"My daughter." Papa smiles. "Watching you wasting away, I had to get help. I left your bedside and ran faster than my chariot's horses to Jesus. I fell at His feet and pleaded for Him to come heal you. But before we got here, our servant met us in the street and said not to bother the teacher because you had died."

"Jesus insisted on coming," Papa adds with tears in his eyes.

I look over at Jesus. "I told your father not to be afraid," He says, "and to believe you would be healed."

"When we arrived, everyone was weeping," Papa says. "Jesus told us to stop crying because you were only sleeping. Everyone laughed at Him, because we knew you were dead."

"But Jesus had the last laugh," I say with a smile.

Jesus' eyes sparkle with delight at my joke. He gives my hand one more squeeze and says, "Get her something to eat."

How does He know I'm so hungry?

New Life

Jesus raised Jairus' daughter from the dead. When you believe in Him, He gives you new life too! He helps you make good decisions, just like the little girl's dad who ran to Jesus to find hope. Trust in Jesus. He gives you a future and a hope.

by Kate Jameson • based on Luke 10:25-37

WHO WILL HELP?

What a *beautiful sunny day,* Zeb thought as he walked to Jericho.

He had heard this road could be dangerous. But today the red, sandstone cliffs shone in the sun. Zeb was enjoying the view so much that he didn't notice a group of robbers. They attacked Zeb, took all his money and left him by the road.

Zeb was all alone. He prayed that God would send help.

Who will help me? he wondered.

Soon a priest walked by.

"Please help me!" Zeb said. He was sure the priest would do something for him.

The priest just looked at him and kept walking.

"Someone else will help you," the priest said. "I can't right now."

A man from Zeb's hometown of Jerusalem came down the road. He looked at Zeb and kept going.

"Wait!" Zeb said.

"I'm sorry," the man said. "I'm just too busy."

A little while later, Zeb saw a Samaritan walking toward him. Jews and Samaritans were enemies. Zeb didn't even bother asking for help. He knew the Samaritan wouldn't stop. But the Samaritan did stop.

"Are you OK?" the Samaritan man asked.

"No," Zeb said. "I've been robbed and badly hurt."

The Samaritan man put bandages on Zeb's injuries and helped him onto his donkey.

Neighbors in Need
Jesus taught that loving your neighbor means helping everyone around you, even people you don't like. How can you help the people around you?

"Thank you," Zeb said.

"I'm not done helping you," the Samaritan man said.

The Samaritan man took Zeb to a nearby inn and paid the owner to take care of him.

"Why did you help me?" Zeb asked.

"I always help my neighbors," the Samaritan said. "No matter who they are."

I'M SO EXCITED TO MEET JESUS!

THERE IS STILL A LOT TO DO!

A BREAK FROM BUSYNESS

by MacKenzie Knoll • based on Luke 10:38-42

Hannah skipped into the house with a huge smile. Jesus and His disciples were on their way to have dinner with her family!

"I'm so excited," Hannah said as Aunt Martha handed her a basket of fruit. "I hope Jesus likes our family recipes."

"There is a lot to do!" Aunt Martha said, wiping sweat from her forehead. "The floor needs to be swept, the table needs to be set and water needs to be drawn from the well."

Hannah loved to help. She got right to work.

When Jesus and the disciples arrived, Hannah was still sweeping. The delicious aromas of fresh bread, lamb and vegetables filled the air as the women put the finishing touches on the meal.

As Hannah swept, she noticed that Aunt Mary wasn't helping at all. She was just sitting and listening to Jesus.

"Aunt Mary, what are you doing?" Hannah asked.

"Just listen to what the Lord says," she said. "He truly teaches the best way to live."

Maybe I should sit and listen to Jesus too? Hannah thought. She went to find Aunt Martha.

"Aunt Martha, can I sit by Aunt Mary and finish sweeping later?" Hannah asked.

Aunt Martha looked at her sister and frowned. "No, we need to make sure everything is perfect for the Lord. I'll ask her to help."

Hannah watched Aunt Martha. She stomped toward her sister and interrupted Jesus.

"Lord, don't You care that my sister has left me to do all the work?" She placed an angry fist on her hip. "Tell her to help me!"

"Martha, Martha," Jesus said. "You are worried and upset about many things. Really, only one thing is needed. Mary has chosen what is better. And it will not be taken away from her."

Aunt Martha and Hannah were quiet as everyone gathered for dinner. After Jesus prayed, they began to pass dishes full of delicious food around the table.

Maybe I should try to be more like Aunt Mary, Hannah thought. *Jesus said it is better to rest and listen to Him than it is to always be busy.*

When they had finished eating, Aunt Martha stood to start clearing the table. Hannah put a hand on her aunt's dress.

"Aunt Martha," she whispered, "maybe we should wait to clean up until Jesus leaves."

Aunt Martha smiled. "That's a great idea, Hannah."

Aunt Mary leaned over and smiled too. "I agree," she said. She squeezed each of their hands.

Hannah squeezed back, not taking her eyes off of Jesus. She couldn't wait to hear what He said.

Learning to Rest

Working hard is important but so is playing with family, taking a nap or spending quiet time with God. Think about how you can use your time wisely. What are some things you can do that will bring you closer to Jesus?

ONE OUT OF TEN

by Christy Hoss • based on Luke 17:11-19

Many months ago, Papa got sick with a skin disease called leprosy. Mama said leprosy could easily spread and couldn't be cured. It made me so sad.

Papa had to go far away to keep us safe. He couldn't hug us when he left. He lived with other lepers. Even if we saw him, we couldn't go near him. Leprosy was a terrible disease! It took away Papa's ability to feel with his hands and feet. He couldn't run fast or hold a spoon to eat.

I thought of Papa all the time and missed him so much.

Today I was helping Mama grind wheat kernels. It was hard work. I looked up to wipe the sweat from my forehead. A man was racing toward me. I rubbed my eyes. It was Papa!

Papa was running with perfectly healed feet. He picked me up in his perfectly healed arms and held me tight.

"Papa!" I cried. "You're all better!"

Mama jumped up and threw her arms around his neck, squashing me in their big hug.

apa stopped hugging us and exclaimed, "I must go back!"

"No, Papa!" I said. "Please don't leave us again." Tears poured down my cheeks.

"I must," he said. "But you can come with me."

Mama and I followed Papa, curious about where he was going.

Up ahead, under the shade trees, a man was talking to other men sitting in a circle. Papa fell to his face in front of the man.

"Thanks be to Jesus the Messiah who healed me from leprosy!" he shouted. "Thank You, Jesus! Thank You, Jesus!"

Wow! It's Jesus, I thought. *The Great Miracle Worker healed my Papa! No wonder he wanted to come back here!*

"Did I not heal 10 lepers?" Jesus asked. "Where are the nine? Didn't anyone else return and give praise to God?"

I was surprised by Jesus' words.

Why didn't the others come back to thank Him? I wondered. *Being healed from leprosy is a miracle!*

Jesus took my papa's hand. "Get up and go," He said. "Your faith has healed you."

Papa lifted me on his shoulders. Having Papa home felt so good.

I want to be just like Papa and have great faith in Jesus, I thought. *I am so thankful for Him.*

Face to Face

Some messages are so important, you have to give them in person. What kind words or thankful feelings can you share with the people closest to you?

THE LIZARD AT THE WELL

SPLASH!

ZZZZ!

Leonard Lizard lay in the sun. He loved his rock beside the well.

Every morning women from the nearby town got water before the day got hot.

Every afternoon Leonard took a nap.

One afternoon Leonard's nap was disturbed by a man who came and sat by the well.

Interesting, Leonard thought. *Men don't come to the well. And nobody comes at this time of day, except for that lonely woman.*

Just then the woman walked up with her clay jars.

"Will you give me a drink?" the man asked.

The woman looked as surprised as Leonard felt. He lifted his head and inched closer.

The man smiled at the woman.

That's strange, Leonard thought. *Nobody smiles at her.*

The woman frowned like she always did.

"How can you ask me for a drink?" the woman said. "Your people don't like my people."

The man kept smiling. "You do not know who is asking you for a drink," He said. "Everyone who drinks this water will be thirsty again. But anyone who drinks the water I give them will never be thirsty. It will flow up into eternal life."

The woman nearly dropped her jug in excitement. "Sir, give me Your special water. Then I won't have to keep coming to the well."

Please give *this* water to her! Leonard cheered. *Then she'll stop disturbing my nap every afternoon.*

The man just laughed. Then He told the woman details about her family that no stranger would know.

"Sir," the woman gasped. "I can see you are a prophet. I know that Messiah is coming. When He comes, He will explain everything to us."

The man stood. "The one you're talking about is the one speaking to you. I am He."

The woman looked happier than Leonard had ever seen her. She spun around and went running into town. She wanted to tell everyone about this amazing man named Jesus.

Soon, many Samaritans came from the town to see Jesus. Everyone gathered and listened to Jesus teach about God. Many believed that He was the Messiah.

"We know that this man really is the Savior of the world," the people said.

Leonard looked around and smiled. "I'm so glad I woke up from my nap for this!"

Caring Kindness

Most people were mean to the Samaritan woman, but Jesus took time to talk with her and be kind. Do you know anyone who might need extra kindness? Think about ways you could show them Jesus' love.

by Frances McFarland • based on John 6:1-14

MIRACLE ON THE MOUNTAIN

The smell of baking bread tickled Nathan's nose. Waking from a deep sleep, he heard the sound of fish sizzling on a fire.

Nathan slid into his sandals and ran into the kitchen.

"Good. You're up!" Mom said. She spread out a cloth and placed five loaves of bread and a couple of fish in the middle. "I heard Jesus is speaking nearby. If we hurry, we can see Him."

Nathan perked up. "Jesus? The man who heals sick people?"

"Some say He is God's Son," Mom said.

"Do you think that's true?" Nathan asked.

"Let's go see for ourselves!" Mom said.

A faint rumble of voices grew louder as they approached a grassy mountainside. When they reached the top of the hill, Nathan saw thousands of people.

Suddenly, a voice rang out above the others. "I can see! Jesus made my blind eyes see!"

Nathan held Mom's hand as they weaved through the crowd. Nobody paid attention to them because everyone was watching Jesus.

"Look, Jesus is lifting a crippled girl to her feet," Mom said.

"She's walking!" Nathan exclaimed.

People cheered when Jesus made sick people well. They carefully listened as He told them wonderful things about God's Kingdom.

Soon lunchtime had passed. Hungry tummies growled. Quiet fell on the crowd as Jesus gathered His disciples. After a quick huddle, the disciples scattered into the crowd. "Does anyone have food?" they called out.

Nathan looked at Mom with big eyes. She smiled and gave him a nod. He sprang to his feet and shouted, "I do!"

One of Jesus' disciples ran over and put a gentle hand on Nathan's shoulder.

"My name is Andrew," he said. "I'll take you to Jesus."

Andrew guided Nathan up the mountainside.

"This boy has food," he reported to Jesus. "But not enough for all these people."

Not even enough for everyone to have a crumb, Nathan thought.

Meeting Jesus

Imagine if you were the boy who gave Jesus the lunch that fed 5,000 people. God's Son still does miracles! On Mother's Day, thank God for moms and all those who teach you about Jesus.

Jesus took Nathan's lunch. He thanked God for the food and began breaking it into pieces. Each time Jesus broke off a piece, there was more!

Nathan's heart pounded with excitement as he ran back to his mother.

"Jesus is so nice and powerful!" he exclaimed.

Minutes later, Nathan and his mom were handed a basket of food. Everyone ate. Then the disciples gathered 12 baskets of leftovers.

"Look at all the extra food." Nathan pointed.

"Jesus cares for sick and for hungry people," Mom said.

"Only God's Son could do miracles like that," Nathan said.

"I believe you're right," Mom said, pulling Nathan into a hug.

by Rachel Pfeiffer • based on John 13:1-17

FOLLOWING in Jesus' FOOTSTEPS

Peter set some bread on the table and sat down. *That should be everything,* he thought.

The disciples had worked hard to get the food and room ready for the Passover feast. Now they could take a break and enjoy the meal together.

"Should we wash our feet?" John asked. Everyone's feet were dirty from a long day of walking and working to get everything prepared.

Peter looked at the empty bowl in the corner of the room. He didn't want to do the job of a lowly worker.

A servant should wash our feet, he thought.

Jesus hadn't talked much that day. The disciples could tell something important was on His mind. Instead of eating, He got up from the table.

Jesus grabbed a towel. Then He filled the bowl with water and knelt in front of Matthew.

Jesus carefully washed Matthew's feet, then John's. Everyone was shocked but didn't know what to say. Next, Jesus came to Peter.

"Lord," Peter said, "are You going to wash my feet?"

Peter knew Jesus was the Son of God. Someone as important as Jesus should not be doing this job.

"**Y**ou don't realize now what I am doing. But later you will understand," Jesus replied.

Peter frowned. "No," he said. "You will never wash my feet."

Jesus looked disappointed. "Unless I wash you, you can't share life with Me," He said.

Oh no, Peter thought. *I said the wrong thing again!*

"Lord," he replied quickly, "not just my feet! Wash my hands and my head too!"

Jesus smiled and shook His head. "People who have had a bath need to wash only their feet. The rest of their body is clean."

Once Jesus had finished washing everyone's feet, He sat at the table again.

"**D**o you understand what I have done for you?" He asked. "You call Me 'Teacher' and 'Lord.' You are right. This is what I am. I, your Lord and Teacher, have washed your feet. So you should also wash one another's feet."

Oh, Peter thought, *I get it now. To be great in God's kingdom, you have to be a servant.*

"Thank You, Lord," Peter said. "Now let's eat."

Hands and Feet

We are Jesus' hands and feet. Jesus showed the disciples that following Him means humbling ourselves to do a job no one else wants to do. It can also mean secretly helping others, even though we won't get noticed. Remember that Jesus sees your service and hard work when no one else does.

A LIFE OF
PRAYER

by Kate Jameson • based on Matthew 6:5-15, 26:36-46

Peter followed Jesus and the other disciples into the garden. Ever since the Passover dinner, Jesus had been acting differently. He seemed sad.

"Peter," Jesus said. "Keep watch with James and John while I go pray."

Jesus was very good at praying. He spent a lot of time talking to His Father and taught all His disciples how to pray well.

Jesus walked farther into the garden. Peter sat down and thought about Jesus' lessons about prayer.

"Don't try to show off with fancy prayers," Jesus had said to a crowd who had gathered on the mountainside. "Pray in your room. Just talk to God. And make sure to listen to what He has to say too."

Jesus told everyone it was important to pray and ask for forgiveness for the times they mess up. He said it was also good to forgive those who treated them badly.

Peter knew Jesus was right. But sometimes Peter got angry. He had a hard time forgiving others . . . and himself.

Peter could hear Jesus praying near him in the garden.

"Father, I know You sent Me to rescue the people You love. I'm scared about what I have to do. But if it's the only way to save everyone, I'll do it."

Peter didn't know what Jesus meant. But he liked how Jesus called God *Father*. Jesus told God everything, even when He was scared.

As Peter listened to Jesus, he slowly drifted off to sleep. Suddenly, he heard Jesus' voice again.

"Can't you stay awake for one hour?" Jesus said.

Great, Peter thought. *I messed up again.*

zzzz

A few days later, a lot had happened. Jesus had been arrested. Peter had denied knowing Jesus. Jesus had been nailed to a cross and placed in a tomb. All the disciples were sad.

"God, why did You take Jesus away from us?" Peter prayed. "I need His forgiveness."

Out of nowhere, several women ran into the room. They had been visiting Jesus' tomb.

"The tomb is empty!" they said. "Jesus is alive again!"

Peter was shocked. He ran to the place where Jesus had been buried. The women were right. The tomb was empty and Jesus had returned!

"Thank You, God," Peter said. "You answered my prayers!"

A Prayer for Life

Prayer allows us to build a relationship with the living God. If you want to know God personally and be forgiven for your sins, you can say this prayer:

"Dear Jesus,
I'm so glad You care about me. I believe You loved me so much that You died on the cross for me. I believe You rose from the dead and can forgive my sins. Please come into my heart and make me Your child.
Amen."

SURPRISE IN THE GARDEN

by Sheryl Ann Crawford · based on Matthew 27:45-28:8

The sky went dark in the quiet garden.

"What happened to the sun?" Baby Bunny asked. "It's only lunchtime."

"Don't be afraid," Papa Bunny said. "I think our Creator is telling the world how He feels."

"The Creator?" Baby Bunny asked. "You mean the One who made cabbages and carrots and bunnies?"

Papa nodded. "God created everything. He has a son named Jesus Christ. Jesus is dying on a cross."

"Dying?" Baby Bunny cried. "No!"

"It's OK," Papa said. "God is in control. He sent His Son to earth to pay the price for the sins of the world."

"You mean all the lying, fighting and selfishness?" Baby Bunny asked.

"Yes," Mama Bunny said. "And much more. Jesus came so sins could be forgiven and people could live with God forever."

RUMBLE BOOM!

Baby Bunny was shocked. Jesus must love the world very much. Suddenly, the ground rumbled in the garden.

Crash! Bang! BOOM!

"Earthquake!" Mama cried.

"Hide under a bush!" Papa said.

The frightened bunnies closed their eyes until the shaking stopped.

"Let's get back to the safety of our den," Mama said.

Not much later, Papa heard noises in the garden. The bunnies stuck their heads outside. They saw a friend of Jesus gently carry His body into a tomb in the garden.

"It is finished," Papa Bunny said sadly.

The rabbit family watched as Jesus' tomb was covered with a big stone.

On the third day, the ground began to shake . . . again. "It's another earthquake!" Baby Bunny cried. This time instead of darkness, a bright light flooded their den. "Stay here!" Papa warned. He carefully poked his head outside to see what was going on in the garden. He saw something that made him freeze in his tracks. "Our Creator has sent a shining angel!" he called. "Come quickly!" The rabbits stared in amazement at the angel sitting on the stone in front of the tomb.

Just then, some women ran up to Jesus' grave.

"Don't be afraid," the angel said to the women. "I know you are looking for Jesus, the One who was killed on the cross. But He isn't here! He has come back to life again, just as He said He would!"

The women shouted with joy. They turned and joyfully ran past the bunnies to tell their friends the wonderful news.

The rabbits leaped at the good news too.

"Did you hear that?" Baby Bunny cried. "Jesus is alive again!"

Perfect Love

When we do things that are wrong, it's called sin. Sin keeps us away from God. When Jesus rose from the dead, He defeated sin. We can only have a close relationship with God by believing in Jesus and asking Him to forgive our sins.

Breakfast on the Beach

by Suzanne Gosselin • based on Luke 22:54-62 and John 21:15-18

The sun sparkled off the Sea of Galilee. Peter and his friends sat on the shore eating breakfast with Jesus.

Then Jesus spoke to Peter. "Do you love Me?"

"You know that I love You," Peter said.

Peter did love Jesus. But he knew his words and actions didn't always show love. He thought of what happened just a few weeks ago.

Peter had been at a garden with Jesus when guards rushed up to them. They arrested Jesus and took Him to the high priest's house.

Peter followed everybody into a courtyard. They built a fire. Peter moved closer and sat down. A woman looked at him and said, "This man was with Jesus."

Peter shook his head. "I don't know Him."

A little while later someone said, "You're one of the disciples."

Peter didn't want to get into trouble. "No," he lied. "I'm not!"

Then another person said, "This fellow must be with Jesus. He's from Galilee."

Peter frowned and lied again. "I don't know what you're talking about!"

Peter would never forget what happened next. A rooster crowed. Jesus turned from the house and looked right at him.

Peter felt ashamed. He ran away and cried.

The next day, Jesus died on a cross. Peter and the other disciples were heartbroken.

But soon, their sadness turned to joy. Jesus had risen from the dead!

Love in Action

Peter put his love for God into action by traveling around and telling people about Jesus. How can you put love into action? Who can you care for today?

"**F**eed My lambs," Jesus said. His words broke into Peter's thoughts. Birds squawked on the beach. The sun made Peter squint.

A second time Jesus asked, "Do you love Me?"

"Yes, Lord," Peter said. "You know that I love You."

Jesus said, "Take care of My sheep."

One more time, Jesus asked, "Do you love Me?"

Peter felt bad that Jesus had asked him again. "Lord, You know all things," he said. "You know that I love You."

Jesus nodded. "Feed My sheep," He said again.

Jesus has given me an important job, Peter thought. *I'll help new believers understand God's great plan.*

Peter had denied Jesus three times. Now he had said "I love you" three times. Jesus was giving him another chance. Peter would use it to prove his love.

JUST WHAT I NeeDeD

by Tim Shoemaker • based on Acts 3:1-10

"Where do you want to sit today?" Isaac asked me.

I sighed. I was more than 40 years old, but I still had to be carried around like a baby. I hadn't walked once since I was born.

"Here is fine," I said.

Isaac set me down near the temple gate called Beautiful. Since I couldn't walk, I didn't have a job. Instead I begged people for money.

"Can you spare some coin?" I cried out.

Most people rushed past, pretending not to see me.
But this morning two men stopped.

"Hello," one man said. "I'm Peter, and this is my friend John."

"Do you have any spare money?" I asked.

Their clothes were ragged, so I wasn't hopeful.

"I don't have any silver or gold," Peter said.

I sighed. Maybe the next person would be able to help me.

"**B**ut I'll give you what I have," Peter added. "In the name of Jesus, walk."

Jesus . . . I'd heard of Him. I knew He had healed many people. I also knew He had died on a cross. Many claimed Jesus had risen from the dead.

As thoughts swirled through my head, Peter took me by the hand. He pulled me to my feet. Instantly my feet and ankles straightened out and filled with strength. I could *walk*!

I jumped around, shouting praises to God! A crowd of people rushed over to see what was going on. They were amazed!

"Why are you surprised?" Peter said to the crowd. "God has done this."

"Praise God!" I shouted.

Peter and John didn't have money to give me, but they gave me something much better. They were kind to me and ended up giving me exactly what I needed—a relationship with Jesus.

More Than Money

You don't need money to help others. How can you do more good and be kind without it costing you anything? Here are a few ideas.
- Give someone a free smile.
- Listen to someone.
- Say something nice to somebody.
- Help somebody get work done.
- Tell somebody about Jesus.

Can you think of other things?

SPEAK UP

by Becky Wilson Suggs • based on Acts 3:1–4:21

"Hurry up, Abner," Dad said. "We don't want to be late for temple."

I ran to catch my family. A beggar sat by the temple gates. The man couldn't walk. He was always there. Even though I couldn't give him any money, I tried to show him kindness with a smile.

As my family left the temple that afternoon, we saw a crowd by the gate. Two men stood with the beggar.

"I don't have money," one man said. "But I'll give you what I have. In the name of Jesus Christ of Nazareth, get up and walk."

The man took the beggar's hand. The beggar stood! Then he started walking, jumping and praising God. It was a miracle!

"How did those men do that?" I asked my dad.

"That's Peter and John," Dad said. "They are followers of Jesus. They say He was the Son of God."

Peter started teaching about Jesus. More people gathered to listen.

"Stop!" a guard's voice shouted. A group of temple guards ran over and arrested Peter and John.

The next day, my family went to see Peter and John stand before the high priests and teachers of the law.

Annas, the high priest, asked lots of questions.

"By what power or what name did you do this?" he asked.

"It is by the power of Jesus' name," Peter said. "You can't be saved by believing in anyone else."

Peter spoke boldly about how Jesus was nailed to a cross but then God raised Him from the dead.

Many people nodded in agreement. I believed too. But the high priest wasn't convinced.

I frowned. The beggar had been healed. God's power had done the impossible. But how could Peter and John prove it?

I knew what I needed to do. I snuck out of the court to find the beggar. If the high priest and others saw the man walking, they would see that Peter and John were telling the truth.

I checked by the gate. He was there!

"**S**ir, you need to come with me," I said.

"Why?" he asked.

"Peter and John need your help," I said.

We hurried back to court. The beggar made his way to the front and stood next to Peter and John.

The high priest and the other leaders recognized the man. They knew he had been born unable to walk. They also knew they couldn't punish Peter and John, because the crowd had seen the miracle.

"We will set you free," they said. "But you can't teach about Jesus anymore."

"We have to obey God and tell others about Him," Peter and John said.

And with that, they were set free.

Taking a Stand

Have you ever seen someone bullied for their faith in Jesus? It can be hard to stand up for someone else, but God promises to always be with us. Deuteronomy 31:6 says, "The Lord your God will go with you. He will never leave you."

From BULLY to BELIEVER

by Kim Washburn • based on Acts 9:1-19

Saul was on a mission. He wanted to stop everyone from following Jesus' teachings. He put Christians in jail and had them beaten.

Saul went on a trip with other Pharisees to tell people to stop believing in Jesus.

"Jesus is not the Messiah," Saul declared.

"That's right!" the other Pharisees agreed.

"Following our laws is more important than doing what Jesus said," Saul continued.

Saul's mind was made up. He believed he was doing the right thing and that Christians were wrong. As he took his next step, a brilliant light flashed. Saul fell to the ground. He heard a loud voice.

SAUL, WHY DO YOU PERSECUTE ME?

"**S**aul, why do you persecute Me?" the voice boomed.

"Who are You, Lord?" Saul asked. He pressed his forehead into the ground.

"I am Jesus, the one you are opposing," the voice said. "Now get up and go into the city. You will be told what you must do."

Saul stood up and tried to brush the dirt from his eyes. He almost fell down again. He was blind!

He reached out shakily. His friends took his hand and led him into the city of Damascus.

When Saul got to the city, he went to his friend's house. He told Judas what happened.

Judas was shocked. "The high priest will know what to do. You should visit him."

Saul thought for a moment. "Jesus said I would be told what to do when I got here. I think I need to pray and wait for Him to speak to me again."

"But I thought you didn't believe in Jesus' teachings," Judas said.

"I may have been wrong about Him," Saul said. "I think He might be exactly who He said He was—the Son of God."

From Saul to Paul
Saul's change was a big one. He changed his name to Paul and traveled to tell people about Jesus. Paul was even put in prison for sharing about Jesus! His letters and writings make up many books in the New Testament. How can you boldly live out your faith like Paul?

Saul prayed and waited. He didn't eat or drink. Three days passed. Then there was a knock at the door.

"Saul, someone is here to see you," Judas said, poking his head in the room.

"Ananias?" Saul asked.

Judas drew a quick breath. "How did you know?"

Saul smiled. "My Savior gave me a vision," he said.

Thump, thump, thump. Saul heard someone come up the stairs.

"Saul," Ananias said, placing his hands on Saul, "Jesus has sent me to help you see again. You will be filled with the Holy Spirit."

Immediately something that looked like scales fell from Saul's eyes. He could see! Saul smiled, blinking back tears.

"I won't try to hurt people who follow Jesus anymore," Saul said. "I will follow what Jesus said and share about His love and forgiveness."

A MIRACLE FOR TABITHA

by Suzanne Gosselin • based on Acts 9:36-42

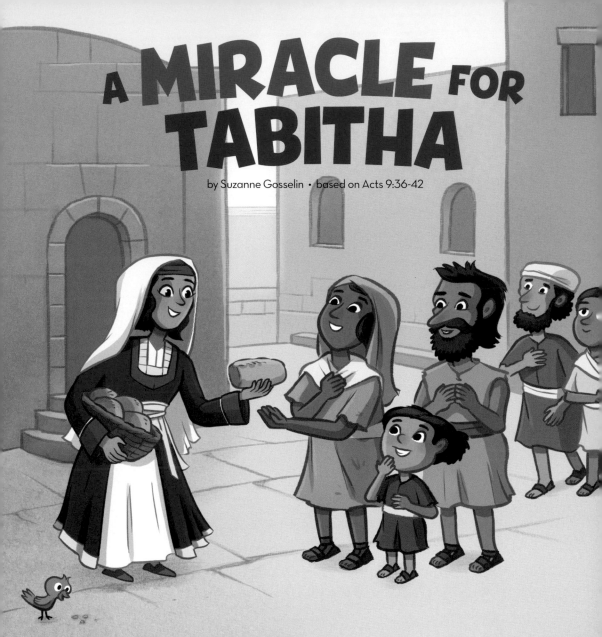

Many people in the city of Joppa knew Tabitha. She was a kind, helpful woman who believed Jesus was God's Son. Tabitha sewed beautiful clothes. She helped the poor. She cared for women whose husbands had died.

Tabitha spent her days serving others, just like Jesus taught. The people loved and appreciated Tabitha, because she was so giving.

One day, Tabitha got very sick and died. Her friends were heartbroken. They laid her on a bed in an upstairs room of her home.

At this same time, a follower of Jesus named Peter was preaching in the nearby town of Lydda.

"Jesus died and rose again to save you from your sins. When you believe in Him, you become a child of God," Peter explained to crowds of people.

Peter did miracles that showed God's power too. When Tabitha's friends heard Peter was nearby, they knew what they needed to do.

Tabitha's friends sent two men to find Peter.

"Please come right away!" the men pleaded. They hoped Peter could help somehow.

Peter followed the men to Tabitha's house. Together they went upstairs. The room was filled with women Tabitha had helped. The women were crying.

"Look at these beautiful robes and clothes Tabitha made for us," they said to Peter.

Peter asked everyone to leave the room. He got down on his knees and prayed. Then he turned to the bed.

"Tabitha, get up!" he said.

Immediately, Tabitha opened her eyes. She looked at Peter and sat up. Peter took her hand and helped her to stand. God had brought Tabitha back to life!

"Everyone, come here," Peter called.

The women and other believers rushed over.

"Praise God!" they said.

The Christians were overjoyed to have their friend back. They quickly spread the news about the miracle God had done throughout the city of Joppa. Lots of people knew of Tabitha and her kindness. When they heard about what had happened, many people believed in Jesus.

Living to Serve

Tabitha's life of service caused people to follow her loving, powerful God too! In 1 Peter 4:10 it says, "Each of you has received a gift in order to serve others. You should use it faithfully." You can be a light for Jesus every day in the good things you do. And that brings glory to God (Matthew 5:16).

THE NEW RULES

by Suzanne Gosselin • based on Luke 22:54-62 and Acts 10

When Jesus went back to heaven, He told His disciples to tell people about Him from one end of the earth to the other. Peter had followed Jesus for years. He was Jewish, one of God's chosen people. But he didn't always do what Jesus said. After Jesus was arrested, Peter told people that he didn't know God's Son. Now Peter wanted to obey Jesus' directions and tell people the Good News. He traveled to Joppa and stayed in a house by the sea.

Forty miles away in a town called Caesarea, Cornelius commanded the Roman army. Cornelius was not Jewish. He was a Gentile. Cornelius had not grown up learning God's Word like Peter had. But Cornelius wanted to know God. He prayed to God and gave to those in need.

One day Cornelius had a dream. An angel told him to send his men to Joppa. "Have them bring back a man named Peter," the angel said.

Cornelius did what the angel said.

Back in Joppa, Peter's stomach rumbled. While he waited for lunch to be ready, he climbed to his rooftop to pray.

God sent Peter a vision. A sheet came down from heaven, carrying all kinds of animals, birds and lizards.

A voice told Peter, "Get up and eat!"

Peter was shocked. Eating any of the animals he saw was against Jewish rules.

"No, I won't!" Peter said. "I've never eaten anything that is not pure and clean."

The voice replied, "Do not say anything is not pure that God has made clean."

Peter understood the message: God's Good News was for everyone—the Jews and the Gentiles.

Suddenly, the sheet went back up into the sky.

ust then, Cornelius' men arrived at Peter's house.

Knock, knock, knock.

When Peter opened the door, the men explained that an angel told Cornelius to bring Peter to him.

Peter invited the men to stay. The next day they all traveled to Cornelius' house. Even though it was against the old rules for Peter to go inside a Gentile's house, he knew that God wanted everyone to know the Good News.

Peter preached that Jesus had died and rose again to save people from their sins. Anyone could believe in Jesus and be forgiven for their sins. Cornelius, his family and his friends believed that day because Peter obeyed God.

Not-So-Secret Identity

God was most important in Peter's life. He wanted everyone to know he was a Christian—a follower of Jesus. Peter prayed to God and told people about Him. Even if people told Peter to stop or made fun of him, he kept sharing about God's love. How can you show others that you follow Jesus and that God loves them?

FAMILY OF FAITH

by Suzanne Gosselin • based on Acts 14:8-20, 16:1-3; 2 Timothy 1:5, 3:14-15

"What happened next?" Timothy asked.

Grandma Lois smiled. "God told Moses to reach out his staff. The Red Sea parted, and God's people walked to the other side on dry ground."

"Weren't they scared?" Timothy wondered.

"I'm sure they were," Grandma Lois said, "but it's important to trust God, especially when you're afraid."

"You can always pray to Him," Timothy's mother added, sitting down beside him. "No matter what's happening, He cares about you and wants to help."

"**W**hy do you worship a God that you can't see?" Timothy's friend asked as they walked home.

"He's the one true God," Timothy answered. "My mom and grandma have taught me about Him for years."

His friend frowned. "It's weird that He doesn't have a temple in Lystra."

Timothy shrugged. Most people in his city didn't follow God. "You can worship God anywhere, not just in a temple," he said.

Timothy waved goodbye to his friend. *I wish more of my friends knew about God,* he thought. *Then I wouldn't feel so lonely.*

Suddenly, he remembered what his mom and grandma said about prayer.

Dear God, please help me be brave and tell other people about You, Timothy prayed.

Timothy learned more and more about God as he grew. One day, a teacher named Paul came to Lystra. He and his friend, Barnabas, preached the Good News about God's Son, Jesus. Timothy and his mother went to listen.

A man who couldn't walk came to hear Paul. Suddenly, Paul stopped talking. Timothy saw him look at the man.

"Stand up on your feet!" Paul said.

The man immediately jumped up. The people were amazed.

"Surely these men were sent by God!" his mother said.

Timothy nodded. "God is so powerful. I want to learn more about Jesus and how He came to save us."

The next time Paul visited Lystra, the believers told Paul that Timothy was a good and faithful Christian. Paul noticed that Timothy knew the Scriptures and believed in God.

"Will you come with me and tell people about Jesus?" Paul asked.

At first, Timothy felt afraid. But he remembered what Grandma Lois said about trusting God.

"Of course I'll come," he said.

Timothy helped preach the good news and encourage many churches. He was a hard worker and became like a son to Paul. Timothy had found exactly what he was born to do.

Know and Grow

Timothy grew up to be a pastor. Paul wrote him two special letters— 1 Timothy and 2 Timothy. In one of his letters, Paul wrote, "I remember your honest and true faith. It was alive first in your grandmother Lois and in your mother Eunice. And I am certain that it is now alive in you also" (2 Timothy 1:5). How does your family help you grow closer to Jesus?

by Rebecca Olmstead • based on Acts 15:36-41

A SECOND CHANCE

JOHN MARK CANNOT COME WITH US THIS TIME!

"No!" Paul said. "John Mark cannot come with us this time!"
John Mark hung his head as he listened at the
doorway. Paul and Barnabas were supposed to be getting ready to
tell more people the Good News of Jesus. Instead they were arguing
about him.

"Don't you remember our first trip?" Paul asked. "John Mark left us
when we needed him. We can't trust him."

"That was last time," Barnabas said.

"We need men who won't run away when things get hard," Paul said.

"You've made mistakes too," Barnabas said. "You got a second
chance. John Mark deserves one too."

Jesus and His followers had stayed with John Mark's family when he was a boy. He could still remember listening closely to the disciples' stories of miracles and healings. Since then, he had wanted to travel with them.

Years later, his cousin Barnabas had a special invitation.

"Come with Paul and me on our trip, John Mark," Barnabas had said. "You can help us."

John Mark was so excited. What a wonderful adventure! He helped Paul and Barnabas as they traveled through Asia and told people about Jesus.

After going to the island of Cyprus, Paul and Barnabas traveled by boat back to the mainland. John Mark decided that he wanted to go home to Jerusalem.

Paul got angry. The missionary journey wasn't done. They still needed John Mark's help. But he left anyway. Ever since, John Mark had regretted that decision.

"There you are!" Barnabas walked over after talking with Paul. He put a hand on John Mark's shoulder. "I have news."

"Paul is right," John Mark mumbled. "I'm not good enough to serve the Lord. I made a terrible mistake."

"We all make mistakes," Barnabas said. "Don't give up."

"But Paul doesn't want me to go on the trip," John Mark said.

"It's all settled," Barnabas said. "You'll come with me to do the Lord's work. Paul will take Silas. We'll go on two trips instead of one."

"Really?" John Mark said. "Thank you, Barnabas! I won't let you down again."

A Chance to Grow

Barnabas gave John Mark a second chance. God does the same for us. Years later, John Mark earned Paul's forgiveness and respect. John Mark became a great church leader. He wrote all about Jesus' life in the Gospel of Mark.

HURRY TO HELP

by Diana Baker • based on Acts 23:12-22

(speech bubble: GREAT RACE, JACOB, YOU'RE FAST!)

"Ready, set, go!"

Jacob raced down the dusty road. His friends Ben and John ran neck and neck with him. With a final burst, Jacob sprinted across the finish line ahead of the others.

"Great race, Jacob," Ben said. "You're fast!"

"Let's race to the temple wall next," John said.

"Go!" Jacob yelled.

Just as the three boys reached the wall, they heard yelling and shouting. They peeked around the corner. More than 40 men were meeting with the chief priests.

One of the men spoke loudly, "We have to convince the town leaders to question Paul."

"Yes," another man said. "When they bring him from prison, we'll ambush him and finish him off."

Jacob looked at his friends with wide eyes.

"That sounds bad," he whispered. "Should we tell someone?"

"I don't know," Ben said. "It's none of our business. Besides, we could get in trouble."

"I'm sure the guards won't let anything bad happen," John said. "Come on, let's go home."

Jacob was quiet while he walked home. *Maybe they're right,* he thought. *But what if something bad happens to that person?*

MAYBE THEY'RE RIGHT.

BUT WHAT IF SOMETHING BAD HAPPENS TO THAT PERSON?

Mom was baking bread when Jacob got home.

"I have a question," he said. "What should you do if you overhear something that might end up with someone getting hurt?"

"You should always stand up to help other people if you can," Mom said. "What did you hear?"

"Some men at the temple want to hurt a prisoner named Paul," Jacob said.

Mom gasped. "Your uncle Paul was arrested for teaching about Jesus."

"Do you think they were talking about him?" Jacob asked.

"He has a lot of enemies, especially at the temple," Mom said.

"I'll go visit him," Jacob said. "I might be able to help."

YOU'RE IN DANGER.

Tough Choices
Paul's nephew really did save his uncle's life that night. Sometimes, it's hard to stand up for other people. But God gives us the courage we need to do what's right. How can you help someone else?

Jacob ran as fast as he could to the prison.

"Why are you here?" Paul asked when he saw his nephew.

"You're in danger," Jacob said.

"But I'm safe in here," Paul said.

"Some leaders are going to trick the chief captain into taking you to the council," Jacob explained. "When you arrive, they're going to attack you."

Paul called a guard. "Please take this young man to the chief captain. He has something important to tell him."

I'M PROUD OF YOU.

The captain nodded when he heard the information. "Thank you," he said. "Go home, and don't tell anyone that you reported this to me."

The next day, Jacob heard that Paul was taken safely out of Jerusalem.

"I'm proud of you," Mom said. "It's not always easy to do what's right."

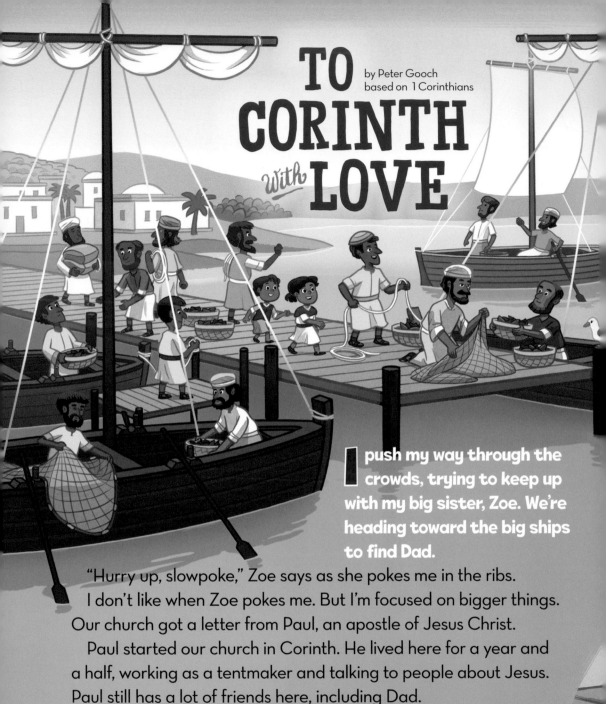

TO CORINTH with LOVE

by Peter Gooch
based on 1 Corinthians

I push my way through the crowds, trying to keep up with my big sister, Zoe. We're heading toward the big ships to find Dad.

"Hurry up, slowpoke," Zoe says as she pokes me in the ribs.

I don't like when Zoe pokes me. But I'm focused on bigger things. Our church got a letter from Paul, an apostle of Jesus Christ.

Paul started our church in Corinth. He lived here for a year and a half, working as a tentmaker and talking to people about Jesus. Paul still has a lot of friends here, including Dad.

Dad still misses Paul. We all do. When Paul moved away, people started arguing. I'm happy Paul wrote us a letter. Maybe it will help everyone get along.

Zoe and I find Dad mending a net near his boat.

"Zoe! Cyrus! What are you doing here?" Dad asks.

"Paul sent the church a letter," I say as I hug him.

"Crispus has it at his house and is going to read it soon," Zoe says.

Dad nods. Hearing this letter is important.

We hurry over to Crispus' house.

Crispus is the ruler of the synagogue. He and his family were some of the first Corinthians who believed in Jesus through Paul's teachings. He knows most of the Christians in our city.

oon after we arrive at his house, Crispus clears his throat and asks for everyone to quiet down. Then Crispus starts reading.

Some of the things in Paul's letter confuse me. Paul mentions milk, bread, meat and being part of one body.

I ask Zoe if she thinks Paul is hungry, but she whispers back, "No, silly. They're just *metaphors*." She pokes me again. I scowl.

Crispus reads on. The next part I understand better: "Love is patient, love is kind. . . . Love never fails."

I know Jesus loves everybody. And Paul obviously loves our church to write such a long letter. Crispus finally gets to the end. I look around the house.

Suddenly, Zoe pokes me again.

"Stop it!" I yell, hitting her hand.

But then I pause. Paul wrote, "Love is patient, love is kind."

Even though we sometimes annoy each other, Zoe and I love each other. That means I should follow Paul's directions. I need to be more patient and kind.

"I'm sorry," I say to Zoe. "I didn't mean to get so mad."

Zoe looks at me. "It's all right," she says. "I'm sorry too. It's not nice to poke you."

I smile and give Zoe a hug. If my sister and I can love each other, maybe the church in Corinth can learn to do the same.

Learning to Love
Love isn't always easy. God calls us to love each other, even when it's hard. Think about some of the people you love. How can you let them know?

Knock, Knock!

by Elaine Tomski
based on Revelation 3:20

Knock, Knock!

Who's there?

Jesus.

Jesus who?

It's Jesus, the only One who knows all about you. I know the good things you do. I also know the bad things you do. No matter what, I love you more than you can ever imagine. You can trust Me.

Knock, Knock!

Who's there?
Jesus.
Jesus who?

It's Jesus, the only One who gives you true forgiveness. All the bad things you do keep you away from God. But I can make you right with God again. I paid for your sins when I died on the Cross. If you ask, I'll forgive you and make your heart clean. You can trust Me.

Knock, Knock!

Who's there?
Jesus.
Jesus who?

It's Jesus, the only One who is always with you. When you look for Me in the Bible, I'll show you what to do. When you pray, I'll listen. With Me, you'll never be alone. You can trust Me.

Knock, Knock!

Who's there?

Jesus.

Jesus who?

It's Jesus, the only One who can always help you. I have power over the whole world. I want to be your Savior and your friend. Will you let Me in? You can trust Me.

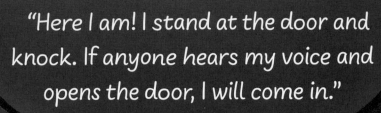

"Here I am! I stand at the door and knock. If anyone hears my voice and opens the door, I will come in."

—Revelation 3:20

If you want to invite Jesus into your heart as your Savior, you can pray this prayer:

"Dear Jesus, thank You for knocking on the door of my heart. Thank You for loving me so much that You died on the Cross to pay for the bad things I do. Please come into my life and make me clean. I want to be Your child and get to know You better. Amen."

KEEP BUILDING YOUR FAMILY'S FAITH

SEE HOW →

MORE SPIRITUAL DISCIPLESHIP

Strong faith is important to you. So help your family live out God's Word with Focus on the Family's faith-building resources!

Focus on the Family Clubhouse Jr.® magazine is full of fun that will reinforce your family's biblical values. Each issue comes with stories, jokes, activities, and more for kids ages 3-7.

Focus on the Family has dozens of resources for children of all ages! No matter what phase of parenting you're in, we have tools for your family's unique journey.

Find everything here:

Scan to explore